FINDING A VOICE:
Women's Fight for Equality in U.S. Society

ORIGINS OF THE WOMEN'S RIGHTS MOVEMENT

LEEANNE GELLETLY

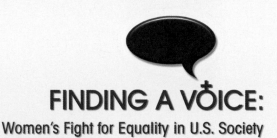

FINDING A VOICE:
Women's Fight for Equality in U.S. Society

TITLES IN THIS SERIES

ORIGINS OF THE WOMEN'S RIGHTS MOVEMENT

LEEANNE GELLETLY

MASON CREST
PHILADELPHIA

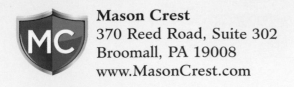

Mason Crest
370 Reed Road, Suite 302
Broomall, PA 19008
www.MasonCrest.com

Printed and bound in the United States of America.

CPSIA Compliance Information: Batch #FF2012-2. For further information, contact Mason Crest at 1-866-MCP-Book.

First printing
1 3 5 7 9 8 6 4 2

Library of Congress Cataloging-in-Publication Data

Gelletly, LeeAnne.
  Origins of the women's rights movement / LeeAnne Gelletly.
     p. cm. — (Finding a voice : women's fight for equality in U.S. society)
  Includes bibliographical references and index.
  ISBN 978-1-4222-2353-6 (hc)
  ISBN 978-1-4222-2363-5 (pb)
  1. Women's rights—United States—History—19th century—Juvenile literature. 2.
Feminism—United States—History—19th century—Juvenile literature. 3. Woman's
Rights Convention (1st : 1848 : Seneca Falls, N.Y.)—Juvenile literature. I. Title.
  HQ1236.5.U6G433 2012
  323.3'40973—dc23

                                        2011043484

Publisher's note: All quotations in this book are taken from original sources, and contain the spelling and grammatical inconsistencies of the original texts.

Picture credits: Boston Public Library: 22; © Lawrence Sawyer/iStockphoto.com: 18; Library of Congress: 8, 12, 13, 16, 19, 20, 21, 25, 26, 29, 32, 35, 36, 37, 40, 41, 43, 44, 45 (top), 49 (center, lower left); 50, 51; National Archives and Records Administration: 49 (top; bottom right), 54; © 2011 Photos.com, a division of Getty Images: 17, 24, 45 (bottom); Jeffrey M. Frank / Shutterstock.com: 34; courtesy Women's Rights National Historical Park, National Park Service: 3, 33.

TABLE OF CONTENTS

INTRODUCTION

A. Page Harrington, director, Sewall-Belmont House & Museum

As the Executive Director of the Sewall-Belmont House & Museum, which is the fifth and final headquarters of the historic National Woman's Party (NWP), I am surrounded each day by artifacts that give voice to the stories of Alice Paul, Lucy Burns, Doris Stevens, Alva Belmont, and the whole community of women who waged an intense campaign for the right to vote during the second decade of the 20th century. The original photographs, documents, protest banners, and magnificent floor-length capes worn by these courageous activists during marches and demonstrations help us bring their work to life for the many groups who tour the museum each week.

The perseverance of the suffragists bore fruit in 1920, with the ratification of the 19th Amendment. It was a huge milestone, though certainly not the end of the journey toward full equality for American women.

Throughout much (if not most) of American history, social conventions and the law constrained female participation in the political, economic, and intellectual life of the nation. Women's voices were routinely stifled, their contributions downplayed or dismissed, their potential ignored. Underpinning this state of affairs was a widely held assumption of male superiority in most spheres of human endeavor.

Always, however, there were women who gave the lie to gender-based stereotypes. Some helped set the national agenda. For example, in the years preceding the Revolutionary War, Mercy Otis Warren made a compelling case for American independence through her writings. Abigail Adams, every bit the intellectual equal of her husband, counseled John Adams to "remember the ladies and be more generous and favorable to them than your ancestors" when creating laws for the new country. Sojourner Truth helped lead the movement to abolish slavery in the 19th century. A hundred years later, Rosa Parks galvanized the civil rights movement, which finally secured for African Americans the promise of equality under the law.

The lives of these women are familiar today. So, too, are the stories of groundbreakers such as astronaut Sally Ride; Supreme Court justice Sandra Day O'Connor; and Nancy Pelosi, Speaker of the House of Representatives.

But famous figures are only part of the story. The path toward gender equality was also paved—and American society shaped—by countless women whose individual lives and deeds have never been chronicled in depth. These include the women who toiled alongside their fathers and brothers and husbands on the western frontier; the women who kept U.S. factories running during World War II; and the women who worked tirelessly to promote the goals of the modern feminist movement.

The FINDING A VOICE series tells the stories of famous and anonymous women alike. Together these volumes provide a wide-ranging overview of American women's long quest to achieve full equality with men—a quest that continues today.

The Sewall-Belmont House & Museum is located at 144 Constitution Avenue in Washington, D.C. You can find out more on the Web at www.sewallbelmont.org

This drawing from the popular magazine *Harper's Weekly*, circa 1859, shows a group of women in a hall listening to a female speaker. During the 19th century it was considered shocking and scandalous for a woman to speak in public to an audience that included men. Yet during the 1850s bold women like Angelina and Sarah Grimké ignored criticism to speak out against the injustice of slavery and to urge greater rights for women.

1

THE RIGHT TO SPEAK

Angelina Grimké stood before the Massachusetts legislature. She wore a simple gray Quaker dress. And she spoke with authority and passion.

A crowd of men filled the room. To be seen, Angelina had to stand at the lectern of the Speaker of the House. Her sister Sarah sat in the Speaker's chair. This was an unusual sight. For in 1838 women did not hold political office. They did not even speak publicly in front of men. Angelina Grimké was defying tradition. She would later tell a friend, "We abolition women are turning the world upside down."

Angelina Grimké was an abolitionist. She wanted to abolish, or end, slavery. The practice of enslaving African Americans had ended in the North. But it remained legal in the South. Abolitionists worked to have laws passed to end slavery throughout the United States. They lectured. They wrote and circulated petitions. And they lobbied lawmakers. But up until Angelina took the podium, only men spoke before government legislators.

SEPARATE SPHERES

In 19th-century America, it was not considered acceptable for women to lecture men. This was especially true in upper- and middle-class homes.

FAST FACT

"In marriage husband and wife are one person, and that person is the husband." This sentence from *Blackstone's Commentaries on English Law* describes a married women's legal status in the United States. In the early 19th century, English common law was the basis for the American legal system.

Men and women's lives were supposed to take place in separate spheres. A man's place was the public sphere. He engaged in business and politics. A woman's place was in the domestic, or private sphere. She was to care for the home, children, and her husband.

This view of a woman's "proper place" was referred to as the "cult of domesticity." A woman was expected to be spiritual. She had to teach her sons and daughters to be moral and virtuous. She was to be a helpmate to her husband. She should never contradict or criticize her spouse. She was to be silent, submissive, and obedient.

Women were considered inferior to men. Many people believed them incapable of learning. Girls seldom received much formal schooling. Women's opinions were often dismissed. In fact, women were not expected to express their ideas at all.

But the abolition movement required political action. Working to change laws brought women into the public sphere. Angelina had chosen to turn the world upside down. For she had to follow her beliefs. But she risked censure for defying society's views.

LECTURING IN PUBLIC

Grimké was not the first woman to speak publicly before men in America. That honor belonged to Frances "Fanny" Wright. Born in Scotland in 1795, Wright came to the United States in 1818. She remained for several years. During that time she lectured as an abolitionist. She also gave talks on women's rights and marriage. People thought her ideas were unusual, and crowds turned out to see her.

In 1828 Wright gave a speech at a fair in New Harmony, Indiana. Both men and women were in the audience. With that lecture, she became the first woman to address a "mixed audience" (a group of men and women). While on a speaking tour, she continued to speak before mixed audiences. She soon became known as "the notorious Fanny Wright."

Most people were outraged at Wright's behavior. The press ridiculed her. Even many women were not supportive. Education reformer Catharine Beecher wrote, "Who can look without disgust and abhorrence upon such an one as Fanny Wright, with her great masculine person, her loud voice, her untasteful attire . . . mingling with men in stormy debate and standing up with bare-faced impudence to lecture to a public assembly?" Later, any woman who spoke in public was scornfully referred to as a "Fanny Wright."

"WE ARE CITIZENS"

Ten years later, abolitionists Angelina Grimké and her sister Sarah risked being called Fanny Wrights. Their appearance before the Massachusetts House of Representatives followed a speaking tour that included mixed audiences. But they ignored criticism. They would do whatever they could to abolish slavery.

In February 1838 Angelina testified that speaking publicly was a moral duty. "I stand before you as a moral being," she told members of the

FAST FACT

Catharine E. Beecher (1800–1878) wrote several books on the "domestic virtues." She also advocated for improved education of girls. Catherine's sister was the novelist Harriet Beecher Stowe.

(Left) This 1829 cartoon mocks Frances "Fanny" Wright (1795–1852), the British-born activist, supporter of female suffrage, and outspoken critic of slavery. Wright's goose head, and the title's reference to her as a "gabbler" alludes to the American lecture tour she conducted that year. Wright caused a national sensation by speaking to audiences composed of both men and women. (Below) This portrait of Wright appeared in a book by Elizabeth Cady Stanton.

House. "And as a moral being I feel that I owe it to the suffering slave to do all that I can to overturn a system of complicated crimes, built upon the broken hearts and prostrate bodies of my countrymen in chains and cemented by the blood, sweat and tears of my sisters in bonds."

Angelina also insisted that women had a right to participate in political affairs. More than 20,000 women had signed the antislavery petitions submitted to the House. They had a right to petition their representatives about slavery, Angelina said. Women were American citizens. She explained "American women have to do with this subject, not only because it is moral and religious, but because it is political, inasmuch as we are citizens of this republic."

RIGHT OF CITIZENSHIP

An American woman in 1838 did not have the same rights as a male citizen. She could not vote or hold political office. She had no voice in

SARAH AND ANGELINA GRIMKÉ

The Grimkés came from a wealthy slave-owning family. Their father was a plantation owner and judge. Sarah Moore Grimké was born in November 1792. Her sister Angelina Emily Grimké was born 13 years later, in February 1805. The sisters grew up in Charleston, South Carolina. Sarah helped care for her younger sister. The two developed a close bond.

Sarah Grimké

After their father died, the sisters freed the slaves they inherited. Sarah left Charleston. By 1821 she was living in Philadelphia. Eight years later, Angelina joined her. Both women converted to the Quaker faith. This religion considers all people equal in the eyes of God. Because of this belief in the equality of all people, Quakers opposed slavery.

Angelina Grimké

Angelina and Sarah became active in abolition work. They assisted in gathering petitions. And they wrote antislavery letters and tracts, or pamphlets. In 1836 they became the first female abolition lecturers in the United States. Both women gained notoriety for speaking publicly at a time when "decent" women did not.

The Grimké sisters lived to see the end of slavery in the United States, which occurred after the Civil War ended in 1865. Sarah Grimké died in 1873. Angelina Grimké died in 1879.

government. She had some legal rights—but only if she was single or widowed. For example, her name could appear on a property deed. She could sign legal contracts or appear in court. But those legal rights disappeared the moment she married.

By law, a married woman's identity was her husband's. A wife could not sign contracts. She could not own property in her name. She did not share guardianship of her children. She did not even own her clothes. She was the property of her husband.

During the 19th century, some women in America began to challenge traditions. Angelina Grimké was one of them. When she spoke to lawmakers in February 1838, she defended the right of all women to be involved in the public sphere. She upheld women's rights to engage in political issues. She even had the audacity to assert that women were citizens.

This small step was the beginning of what would be a long journey on the road for women's rights. In daring to speak, the Grimké sisters inspired many women to examine their own lack of rights as citizens of their nation.

2

REFORMING SOCIETY

I n the early 1800s industrial growth was changing the United States. Steamboats and railroads linked cities. Factories sprang up in the North. People moved from farms to cities. And more and more immigrants settled in urban areas.

As city populations grew, so did concerns about social problems. With urban growth came rising rates of poverty, crime, and disease. Most people could not read or write. And there was growing violence.

Many Americans knew something had to be done, and they wanted to help. Some people founded schools for the poor. Others established aid societies to raise funds for orphanages. And still others provided places where the elderly could live.

Some aid groups were part of religious organizations. Others were volunteer organizations. Many middle-class and wealthy women joined these groups. Such work was open to women, and even encouraged, because it was considered to be within the domestic sphere.

REFORM MOVEMENTS

Several reform movements arose during the 1800s. To *reform* something can mean to rebuild or improve it. Education reformers knew the school system in America was not working. They wanted to improve the educational

During the 1800s, industrial growth and immigration to the United States led to crowded cities and many social problems. Reformers—many of whom were women—wanted to improve the lives of Americans by providing better schools, improving living conditions, and eliminating slavery.

system and help more children get schooling.

Other people believed that poverty and violence resulted from drunkenness. They wanted to improve the lives of American families. To prevent men from drinking, they called for outlawing the sale of alcoholic beverages. These reformers were part of the temperance movement.

The word *reform* can also refer to eliminating an injustice. During the 19th century, the existence of slavery was seen as a great injustice by many people, especially in the northern states. Whites and free blacks formed societies with different goals. Some groups tried to purchase slaves from their owners. Others believed that blacks should be freed and then sent to a colony in Africa. Abolitionists called for an immediate end to slavery. They wanted to see the practice outlawed. All these reformers belonged to the antislavery movement.

Women joined many reform movements. But they usually did not work alongside men. Instead, they formed separate groups made up of only women. Only women belonged to these organizations. They ran their own meetings, and they gave lectures before other women's groups. Sometimes women attended the men's reform meetings, but they usually were not allowed to speak.

EDUCATIONAL REFORM

Educational reformers saw that the nation needed more schools. There were some private schools. But poor students could not afford to attend them. Reformers lobbied states to create free public schools so the poor could get an education. Their work was successful. The early decades of the 1800s saw the founding of many public schools.

By the middle of the century, most northern states had public elementary school systems. This gave white children access to a formal education. Some states also funded high schools. But almost all colleges and preparatory schools were closed to women.

In some areas of the United States, girls were not allowed to attend public schools with boys until the 1840s. Instead, young women attended all-girl schools. These schools traditionally emphasized subjects like deportment, sewing and embroidery, music, religion, and drawing over academic subjects.

HIGHER EDUCATION

At the beginning of the century, girls had limited educational opportunities. Few schools allowed them to enroll. Existing schools had low academic standards, and girls learned mostly domestic skills.

Between 1820 and 1850, women's education improved. Numerous academies and seminaries were established. Most were for girls. They provided a high school–level education. And they featured classes to train teachers. In 1821 Emma Hart Willard founded the Troy Female Seminary in New York. Two years later Catharine and Mary Beecher set up the Hartford Seminary in Connecticut. In 1828 Mary Lyon and Zilpha Grant founded the Ipswich Female Seminary in Massachusetts.

In 1837 women could finally attend college. That year Mary Lyon founded the first four-year college for women. Mount Holyoke Seminary

Mount Holyoke, pictured above, was the first of a group of historically women's colleges founded between 1837 and 1889 that are known as the "Seven Sisters." The other colleges include Barnard, Bryn Mawr, Radcliffe, Smith, Vassar, and Wellesley. All are still in existence, although Radcliffe is now part of Harvard University and Vassar admits both men and women.

was located in Massachusetts. The school set a high level of academic standards. It would serve as a model for several future women's colleges.

Another college accepting girls was Ohio's Oberlin College. It opened its doors in 1833. And in 1837 it began accepting women. Oberlin was the nation's first coeducational school of higher learning. The first women to receive bachelor's degrees in the United States earned them at Oberlin.

Many seminary and college graduates became teachers. Some went on to found new schools. Teaching became one of the few careers open to women. School boards were happy to hire female teachers. Their salaries were half the amount paid to male teachers.

THE TEMPERANCE MOVEMENT

In 1826 the American Temperance Society was founded in Boston, Massachusetts. It soon had branches across the country. By the mid-1830s, it had more than 200,000 members.

Reform work involved educating people about the problems caused by alcohol. Temperance supporters wrote tracts and hired speakers. They lobbied state legislatures to impose taxes on liquor. And they petitioned to change laws.

Thousands of women joined the temperance movement. They supported efforts to loosen divorce laws. They wanted states to permit divorce if husbands abused alcohol. Another major goal was to outlaw the sale of liquor everywhere. Efforts at prohibition gradually succeeded. In 1851 Maine would be the first state to ban alcohol.

DAUGHTERS OF TEMPERANCE

This Currier and Ives illustration from the 1840s promotes the Daughters of Temperance, a national organization of women that worked for laws restricting the consumption of alcohol.

THE ABOLITIONIST MOVEMENT

England had banned the international slave trade in 1807. The United States followed in 1808. But white Southerners refused to outlaw slavery. They believed it was essential to the region's agricultural economy. Slaves worked to raise and harvest crops that could be sold for a profit. These included cotton, tobacco, rice, and hemp.

This illustration of a chained slave, with its banner reading "Am I Not a Man and a Brother?," appeared on an 1837 American Anti-Slavery Society publication.

Abolitionists believed slavery was a sin. One of the movement's most outspoken leaders was William Lloyd Garrison. In 1831 he founded an antislavery newspaper called *The Liberator*. In 1833, with Arthur Tappan, he established the American Anti-Slavery Society (AAS). In early December 1833, the Society held its first convention. It took place in Philadelphia.

At the convention was a Quaker woman named Lucretia Mott. Mott belonged to the Hicksite Quakers. This group strongly opposed slavery. Hicksite Quakers boycotted any goods produced by slave labor. These included cotton and cane sugar. During the 1830s Lucretia frequently spoke out against slavery at Quaker gatherings.

FAST FACT

A free black woman named Maria Stewart was one of the first lecturers against slavery. In the early 1830s, she gave speeches to African-American audiences in Boston. She spoke against slavery and racial inequality, and she called for educational and job opportunities for African Americans.

Because of Mott's powerful gift as an orator, she was recognized as a Quaker minister. At the antislavery convention, she asked to speak. Her words moved the crowd.

FEMALE ANTI-SLAVERY SOCIETIES

Only black and white men belonged to the AAS. So Mott could not be a member. But a few days after its founding, she set up a separate organization. The Philadelphia Female Anti-Slavery Society was also founded in

LUCRETIA MOTT (1793–1880)

Lucretia Coffin was born on Nantucket Island, Massachusetts. Her parents were Quakers. Lucretia's father was often away at sea. So Lucretia often saw her mother take charge of business and family matters. The young girl grew up believing in human equality. Lucretia and her sister Martha attended the same Quaker schools as boys.

In 1811 Lucretia married James Mott. They moved to Philadelphia, where James worked as merchant. Lucretia raised five children. She also taught part-time in a Quaker school. By 1821 she was recognized as a Quaker minister.

Both Lucretia and James became active in the abolitionist case. She became a renowned speaker. She also became a strong proponent of women's rights. Mott would later say she "grew up so thoroughly imbued with woman's rights that it was the most important question" of her life.

Until her death in 1880, Mott played a major role in the woman suffrage movement. She spoke at women's rights conventions. And she remained active in the efforts to promote women's rights as well as rights for African Americans.

FAST FACT

In 1840 the American Anti-Slavery Society had an estimated 130,000 to 170,000 members. There were more than 1,600 chapters across the country.

December 1833. Both black and white women made up its 60 members.

Soon there were many other female antislavery societies. Maria Weston Chapman founded the Boston Female Anti-Slavery Society. Similar organizations sprang up in other New England towns. Societies could also be found in New York and Pennsylvania.

Female antislavery societies promoted the cause in many ways. They raised funds at antislavery fairs. They wrote and delivered speeches against slavery. They participated in boycotts of slave labor goods. And they provided support for escaped slaves.

In 1840, abolitionist Maria Weston Chapman (1806–1885) was one of three women chosen for a position on the executive committee of the American Anti-Slavery Society. (The others were Lydia Child and Lucretia Mott). At the time, the appointment of women to positions of leadership in an organization made up of both male and female members was extremely controversial.

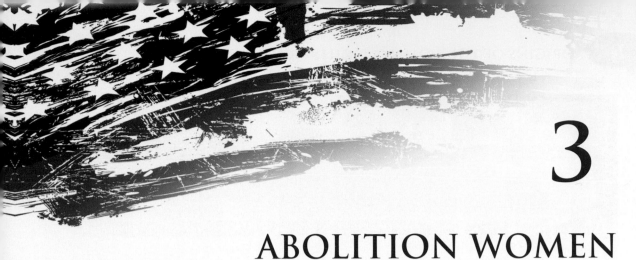

3

ABOLITION WOMEN

Like other reform organizations, the American Anti-Slavery Society published tracts. It hired speakers, and its antislavery newspapers published articles and letters. But abolition was unpopular in much of the North, as well as the South. Promoting the cause could be dangerous. When abolitionists lectured, they ran the risk of being attacked for voicing their thoughts publicly. Many of them were pelted with angry words and rotten fruit. One newspaper publisher was murdered. But the speakers did not stop.

PETITIONING

An important part of abolition work was petitioning. Campaign organizers targeted specific neighborhoods. Volunteers stopped in each home of a specific area. They talked about the reform movement. They asked people to oppose slavery. People supporting abolition signed petitions to show their support of the cause. These documents were submitted to state and national legislatures.

Women did the bulk of antislavery petitioning. They were very successful. During the 1830s, their paperwork swamped Congress. "There would be but few abolition petitions if the ladies . . . would let us alone," complained one congressman. To stop the flood, the U.S. House of Representatives instituted a "gag rule." The rule, which was passed in May 1836,

In the 1830s the U.S. House of Representatives passed a "gag rule" that limited debate on the subject of slavery. The legislative body soon received a large number of petitions about other issues. Many of these were submitted by people who were angry about being denied the right to ask their government to take action against slavery.

meant that Congress would not pay attention to petitions on the subject of slavery.

WOMEN ABOLITION AGENTS

Among the women who helped with petitioning were Sarah and Angelina Grimké. They also wrote and distributed pamphlets. Angelina wrote *Appeal to the Christian Women of the South*. It urged Southern women to free any slaves they owned. The AAS published the 36-page tract in 1836.

The sisters' writings impressed the group's leaders. William Lloyd Garrison, Henry Stanton, Lewis and Arthur Tappan, and Theodore Weld asked the women to be agents. Agents traveled on behalf of the Society. They lectured groups to convert them to the abolitionist cause. The Grimkés were Southerners who had grown up with slavery. They had first-hand knowledge of its horrors.

Angelina and Sarah accepted. In December 1836 they became the first women to lecture for the American Anti-Slavery Society.

At first the Grimkés spoke to groups in private homes. These talks took place in the state of New York. But many women wanted to hear the sisters. They needed bigger meeting places. Some ministers offered their

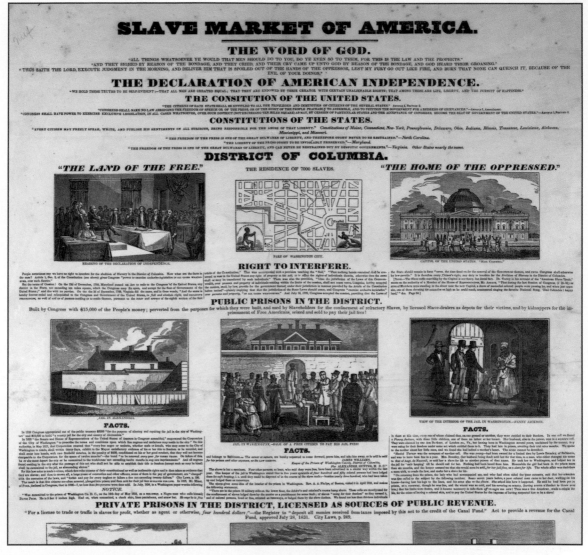

This American Anti-Slavery Society publication from 1836 condemns the sale of slaves in the District of Columbia. Issued as part of a petition campaign asking Congress to abolish slavery in the capital district, the text contains arguments for abolition and stories about the harsh treatment of slaves in the district. At the top are two contrasting scenes: a view of the reading of the Declaration of Independence, captioned "The Land of the Free," with a scene of slaves being led past the Capitol Building, entitled "The Home of the Oppressed." Between them is a street plan of Washington, D.C.

church halls. These rooms also filled up. During the spring of 1837 the Grimkés gave talks throughout New York State.

FIRST ANTI-SLAVERY CONVENTION OF AMERICAN WOMEN

In May 1837 the first Anti-Slavery Convention of American Women took place in New York City. More than 200 women, black and white, attended. They came from 10 states. The meeting was the first public political meeting of women in the United States. It was also the first major interracial gathering.

Lydia Maria Child (1802–1880) was an educator, writer, and abolitionist.

Most abolitionist groups were either all white or all black. The American Anti-Slavery Society and the Female Anti-Slavery Societies of Philadelphia and Boston were integrated. White leaders included Maria Weston Chapman, Lydia Maria Child, Abby Kelley, and Lucretia Mott. Sarah and Angelina Grimké also attended the convention. A small portion of the women were African Americans. They included Sarah M. Douglass, Grace Douglass, Maria Stewart, and Sarah L. Forten.

The women called for ending slavery in Washington, D.C., and in the territory of Florida. They organized a petition campaign. Their goal was to collect a million signatures.

A WOMAN'S NATURAL CHARACTER

After the convention, the Grimké sisters continued their speaking tour in New England. Each week they spoke at five or six meetings. As they traveled from town to town, they attracted large crowds. Men began attending the lectures, too. Soon the sisters were speaking to "mixed" audiences. Women's rights had also become a regular topic.

Members of the New England clergy were appalled. In July 1837, the ministers issued a Pastoral Letter. It did not name the Grimkés. But it rebuked women who lectured in public. "The appropriate duties and influence of women are clearly stated in the New Testament," the letter said. "Those duties and that influence are . . . private." It warned that when a woman "assumes the place and tone of man as a public reformer . . . her character becomes unnatural."

ADVOCATING EQUALITY

Sarah Grimké answered the Pastoral Letter by publishing her views on women. They appeared in a series of letters published in newspapers.

ABBY KELLEY FOSTER (1811–1887)

Abby Kelley was born on January 15, 1811. Raised a Quaker, she grew up near Worcester, Massachusetts. After attending a local school, Abby went to a Quaker boarding school in Providence, Rhode Island. Afterward, she became a schoolteacher.

In 1836 Kelley moved to Lynn, Massachusetts. There, she became a member of the Lynn Female Anti-Slavery Society. She met the Grimkés when they toured New England. Their speeches inspired her to become a lecturer.

In 1838 Kelley was hired as an agent for the American Anti-Slavery Society. She would lecture for the group for the next 20 years. By 1850 she was also speaking in favor of women's rights. Some crowds grew angry at her blunt and fiery rhetoric. Others ridiculed her for sharing the stage with black lecturers. Among those speakers were Frederick Douglass, Sojourner Truth, and Frances Ellen Watkins Harper.

In 1845 Abby married abolitionist Stephen Foster. The couple had a daughter in 1847. She continued to work as a lecturer and fundraiser for the Anti-Slavery Society. She also helped train antislavery lecturers. Two of them, Lucy Stone and Susan B. Anthony, would be future leaders of the women's rights movement.

Sarah protested the low value put on women and their work. She decried women's lack of access to higher education. She noted women's limited opportunities to earn a living.

Sarah called for full equality for women. "I ask no favors for my sex. I surrender not our claim to equality," she said. "All I ask of our brethren is, that they will take their feet from our necks, and permit us to stand upright on that ground which God designed us to occupy."

In 1838 the letters were published in a book. It was entitled *Letters on the Equality of the Sexes and the Condition of Woman*. Future feminist leaders would refer to the book as they worked for women's rights. Some historians have called it one of the founding documents of the women's rights movement.

A LACK OF RIGHTS

Angelina Grimké also responded to criticisms. Education reformer Catherine E. Beecher reprimanded the Grimkés for speaking before mixed audiences. Angelina defended a woman's right to speak. In a private letter to Theodore Weld she insisted antislavery work required it. "What then can woman do for the slave when she is . . . shamed into silence?"

Angelina also wrote a series of letters. In one of the letters she noted similarities between women and slaves. Both had no rights. "The investigation of the rights of slaves," Angelina wrote, "has led me to a better understanding of my own." The letters appeared in antislavery newspapers. In 1838 they were published in a book entitled *Letters to Catherine Beecher*.

FAST FACT

Although slavery had been outlawed in the North, many northern whites opposed the idea of equality between blacks and whites. Some cities and states passed laws establishing separation of the races.

SECOND ANTI-SLAVERY CONVENTION OF AMERICAN WOMEN

In the spring of 1838 the Grimkés were back in Philadelphia. That May Angelina married Theodore Weld. He wanted to ensure that marriage would not take away his wife's rights. So Weld renounced the law that gave him legal ownership of her.

The day after the wedding, Angelina spoke at the second Anti-Slavery Convention for American Women. The Philadelphia meeting attracted around 3,000 people. They were white and black, male and female. But outside the hall was an angry white mob of about 17,000. They were angry over the mixing of genders and races.

The noise of the unruly mob drowned out the speakers. Rocks crashed through windows. Abolitionist Maria Weston Chapman could not be heard. Angelina Grimké Weld managed to speak next. Her hour-long lecture calmed the nervous audience. Afterward, whites and blacks exited the building together.

But the mob was not done. The next day it came back. Rioting men broke into the building and set it on fire. It burned to the ground.

A angry mob destroys Pennsylvania Hall, which had been built in Philadelphia as a place for abolitionists to meet. It was burned to the ground in May 1838—just a few days after construction on the building was finished.

FAST FACT

After they retired from lecturing, Angelina and Sarah Grimké helped Theodore Dwight Weld compile information for his 1839 book *American Slavery as It Is: A Testimony of a Thousand Witnesses*. Harriet Beecher Stowe used some stories from this book when she wrote her 1852 novel *Uncle Tom's Cabin*. The bestselling antislavery book added to the negative view of slavery that was growing in the nation.

After the 1838 convention, the Grimké sisters no longer lectured for the antislavery effort. Health problems cut short Angelina's lecturing work. But another woman soon took her place.

Abby Kelley had also been at the 1838 antislavery convention. It was there that she gave her first speech to a mixed audience. The fury of the mobs did not frighten her. Kelley passionately believed in the need to end slavery. Audience flocked to her stirring antislavery lectures.

DIVISION

Some male members of the AAS did not approve of women lecturing in public. And they did not want women to talk about women's rights. These men feared that women were drawing attention from abolition.

In 1839 the third and final Anti-Slavery Convention of Women met in Philadelphia. Soon after, the American Anti-Slavery Society voted to allow women as members. Lucretia Mott and Abby Kelley were appointed to lead committees. Some men refused to accept them. Led by Arthur Tappan, they broke away. Their formed a new organization. It was named the American and Foreign Anti-Slavery Society. William Lloyd Garrison continued to head the AAS. An early supporter of women's rights, he welcomed women in the organization.

4

SENECA FALLS

In June 1840 members of the American Anti-Slavery Society traveled to London, England. They planned to attend the World Anti-Slavery Convention. In the group were Lucretia and James Mott. Newly married Henry Brewster Stanton was accompanied by his 25-year-old wife, Elizabeth Cady Stanton.

WORLD ANTI-SLAVERY CONVENTION

There were eight women in the AAS delegation. All of them were denied the right to participate. Lucretia Mott later wrote that male abolitionists feared women at the meeting "would lower the dignity of the convention." The women were refused a seat on the floor. They had to sit instead in a curtained balcony.

William Lloyd Garrison arrived late. When he saw the women would not be seated, he refused to participate. He joined the women in the balcony.

Lucretia Mott and Elizabeth Cady Stanton had not met before. But they quickly bonded. They found they held many similar views. Stanton would later write, "As Mrs. Mott and I walked home, arm in arm, commenting on the incidents of the day, we resolved to hold a convention as soon as we returned home, and form a society to advocate the rights of women."

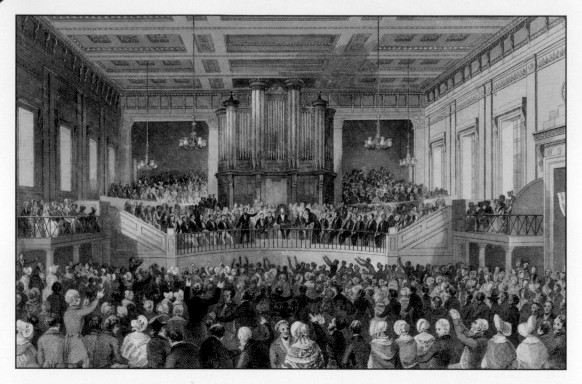

This 1841 illustration purports to show delegates to the World Anti-Slavery Convention, held in London in June 1840. Women were not permitted to sit on the front platform with the other participants, but were restricted to balcony or audience seats.

But Stanton and Mott did not act right away. Elizabeth became involved in raising her family. By 1848 she and her husband had three young sons. The Stantons were living in upstate New York. Their house was in the small town of Seneca Falls. During the 1840s Lucretia Mott was also busy. She lectured at Quaker Meetings on the issue of slavery. She also addressed the Pennsylvania, New Jersey, and Delaware state legislatures.

TEA PARTY

In the summer of 1848, Mott visited her sister in Waterloo, New York. Martha Wright's home was not far from Seneca Falls. Lucretia and Elizabeth made arrangements to meet for tea at the home of Jane Hunt in Waterloo.

On July 13 five women gathered at the Hunt home. Jane Hunt, Mary Ann M'Clintock, Lucretia Mott, Martha C. Wright, and Elizabeth Cady Stanton had much in common. All were activists. But their reform work had encountered many of the same obstacles. They were barred from meetings. Their work was not considered equal to that of men. As women, they were second-class citizens.

The group agreed that women in America deserved better. It was decided to hold a convention on women's rights. Two days later, Stanton placed an advertisement in the *Seneca County Courier*. The ad invited people to attend "A Convention to discuss the social, civil and religious condition

In 1848 Thomas and Mary Ann M'Clintock lived in this two-story house in Waterloo, New York. It was here that Jane Hunt, Mary Ann M'Clintock, Lucretia Mott, Martha C. Wright, and Elizabeth Cady Stanton met in July 1848 to draft what they called the "Declaration of Sentiments." A few days later, the document would be presented publicly at the Woman's Rights Convention in nearby Seneca Falls.

One of the original walls of the Wesleyan Chapel on Fall Street in Seneca Falls, where the Seneca Falls Woman's Rights Convention was held in July 1848. Preservation work on the structure, which is part of Women's Rights National Historical Park, began in August 2009.

and rights of woman." Word spread that Lucretia Mott, a respected voice in the antislavery movement, would be speaking.

On July 19, the meeting convened. Approximately 300 people gathered in the Wesleyan Methodist Chapel in Seneca Falls. Among them were 40 men.

After being introduced by Elizabeth, Lucretia Mott stated the reasons for holding the convention. Then she gave a lecture on the importance of education for women. Stanton took the stage next. It was her first time speaking publicly. At first she spoke so softly that many people had difficulty hearing her. But the words in the document she had written would resound across the nation.

DECLARATION OF SENTIMENTS

Stanton read aloud from the Declaration of Rights and Sentiments. She had modeled the document on the Declaration of Independence. The first line of the Revolutionary War document states that all men are created equal. The first line of the Declaration of Sentiments reads, "We hold these truths to be self-evident, that all men and women are created equal."

The Declaration of Independence contains 18 grievances against King George III of England. Similarly, the Declaration of Sentiments listed 18 injustices against men. Some of the grievances noted women's lack of political rights and privileges. They described women's limited educational opportunities. And they complained of unfair wages for women's work. To correct these wrongs, the document proposed several actions. They were written as 11 resolutions.

On the second day of the convention, the delegates voted on the declaration and its resolutions. The Declaration of Sentiments was adopted unanimously. Then each resolution was voted upon separately. The ninth

ELIZABETH CADY STANTON (1815–1902)

Elizabeth Cady was born on November 12, 1815, in Johnstown, New York. She grew up in a wealthy family. Her father, Daniel Cady, was a judge. Elizabeth had an advanced education for a girl. She studied Greek, Latin, and mathematics at Johnstown Academy. She attended Troy Female Seminary. And she studied the law books in her father's office.

After graduating in 1832, Elizabeth became involved in the antislavery movement. In 1840 she married abolitionist Henry Stanton. She felt strongly even then about women's legal rights. She refused to include the word "obey" in her wedding vows.

After meeting Lucretia Mott, Stanton became inspired to work for women's rights. She would spend decades writing and lecturing for woman's suffrage. But Stanton also campaigned for women's property rights, divorce law reform, and temperance. Much of Elizabeth Cady Stanton's reform work was conducted in partnership with Susan B. Anthony.

resolution startled some attendees. It demanded suffrage for women. It stated that women should have the right to vote: "Resolved, that it is the duty of the women of this country to secure to themselves their sacred right to the elective franchise."

THE RIGHT TO VOTE

Many people considered the idea too radical. Stanton later wrote that Lucretia protested when Elizabeth included the suffrage resolution. "But I

Former slave Frederick Douglass (1818–1895) spoke at the Seneca Falls Convention. He encouraged the delegates to endorse the ninth resolution of the Declaration of Sentiments, which demanded that American women be granted the right to vote.

persisted," Stanton explained, "for I saw clearly that the power to make the laws was the right through which all other rights could be secured."

One speaker who helped the suffrage resolution pass was Frederick Douglass. The former slave was a lecturer for the American Anti-Slavery Society. Just 10 years earlier he had escaped from slavery in Maryland. He now lived in nearby Rochester, New York. He published an antislavery newspaper, the *North Star*.

Douglass was in favor of suffrage for women. And he shared his approval in a speech before the convention. He insisted that women had a right to participate in government. The words of the former slave helped sway the attendees. The suffrage resolution passed. But the vote was not unanimous.

Ultimately all 11 resolutions were adopted. The Declaration of Sentiments was then signed by 100 people. With their signatures, 68 women and 32 men gave their public support to women's rights.

Margaret Fuller (1810–1850) was a journalist and women's rights advocate in the areas of education and employment. Her most famous work is *Woman in the Nineteenth Century*, published in 1845. Fuller influenced many of the early leaders of the women's rights movement, including Susan B. Anthony and Elizabeth Cady Stanton.

ROCHESTER CONVENTION

Two weeks later, women in Rochester hosted another convention. Lucretia Mott again served as a speaker. Many people from the Seneca Falls convention were present.

At the meeting both Mott and Stanton had trouble breaking with tradition. At the Seneca Falls Convention, men had chaired the meeting. (James Mott and Thomas M'Clintock had presided.) But Abigail Bush explained that she planned to run the Rochester meeting. Both Lucretia and Elizabeth were opposed. They worried that Bush had no experience running a public meeting. But the idea was put to a vote and approved. Abigail Bush went on to preside over the convention. She had no problems. It was the first time a woman chaired a meeting with a mixed audience.

A NEGATIVE REACTION

Antislavery newspapers such as Frederick Douglass's *North Star* wrote positively about the Seneca Falls Convention. But other newspapers ridiculed the idea of women being equal to men. They mocked the Seneca Falls participants. The *New York Herald* joked that a woman might run for U.S president. Some people who signed the Declaration of Sentiments withdrew their names from the document.

Many members of the clergy also denounced the idea of women's equality. Ministers preached that the Bible called for women to be subordinate to men. Lucretia Mott commonly challenged biblical interpretations. In

FAST FACT

In 1839 Mississippi was the first state to pass a Married Woman's Property Act. A few months before the Seneca Falls Convention, in 1848, New York passed a similar law. Both laws gave women legal ownership of property brought to marriage.

her lectures, she pointed to passages in the Bible that supported the idea of women's independence.

DISCOURSE ON WOMAN

In December 1849 Mott delivered a speech in response to essayist Richard H. Dana, Sr. She had attended his lecture "Address on Woman," in Philadelphia. Dana condemned women who spoke in public. And he criticized those who demanded women's rights.

Lucretia Mott presented a speech defending women reformers. She insisted that women deserved the same rights as men. This included the right to suffrage. And she insisted that married women had a right to their property and income. It was wrong that a woman was "degraded into a mere dependent," she said.

Discourse on Woman was printed in pamphlet form in 1850. The tract would be distributed in many women's rights conventions in the years that followed.

5

WORKING FOR CHANGE

Reformers set out to change society's attitudes and laws. The Declaration of Sentiments outlined a basic plan. They were to "employ agents, circulate tracts, petition the State and national Legislatures, and endeavor to enlist the pulpit and the press in [their] behalf." Some of this work would be done at conventions.

FIRST NATIONAL WOMAN'S RIGHTS CONVENTION

About a thousand people attended the first National Woman's Rights Convention. It took place in Worcester, Massachusetts, in October 1850.

The event's principal organizer was antislavery activist Paulina Wright Davis. She invited many speakers. They included Lucretia Mott, Abby Kelley, Lucy Stone, William Lloyd Garrison, and Frederick Douglass. Family demands kept Elizabeth Stanton at home. But she included her name as a sponsor. Davis presided over the meeting.

Lucy Stone helped organize the convention. When she spoke, she urged participants to petition their state legislatures. There were two main goals for women's rights reformers. Women needed suffrage. And married women needed legal recognition of their right to own property.

A WOMAN BEFORE AN ABOLITIONIST

Lucy Stone was an early convert to speaking for women's rights. She was an 1847 graduate of Oberlin College. Subsequently she became a fiery orator for the Massachusetts Anti-Slavery Society. She came to the conclusion that women were oppressed in the same way as slaves. So her antislavery talks included support for women's rights.

The Anti-Slavery Society reprimanded Lucy for speaking on women's issues. She refused to stop. "I was a woman before I was an abolitionist,"

LUCY STONE (1818–1893)

Lucy Stone was born August 13, 1818, near West Brookfield, Massachusetts. After graduating from Oberlin College in 1847, she became a lecturer for the Massachusetts Anti-Slavery Society. She also delivered impassioned appeals for women's rights. Many members of the woman's movement would say they joined after hearing Lucy. They include writer Julia Ward Howe and author Helen Hunt Jackson.

In May 1855 Stone married abolitionist Henry Browne Blackwell. She opposed unjust marriage laws. So the couple renounced laws that gave the husband legal right to claim his wife's property and wages. Stone also did not take Blackwell's name. She is the first recorded American woman to keep her maiden name after marriage.

Stone lectured during most of the 1850s. She was so successful that she could support her family on money from lecture fees and donations. After the loss of her second child 1859, Lucy withdrew from public speaking.

In the late 1860s Lucy would once more become a force in the women's rights movement. And she would remain active in the movement until her death in October 1893.

she told them. They compromised. It was agreed that Stone would be paid by the Society for giving antislavery lectures on weekends. During the week she was free to lecture on women's rights at her own expense.

Stone attracted thousands of people at a time to her lectures. One newspaper reported, "Wherever she goes the people en masse turn out to hear Lucy Stone, and are never weary of her stirring eloquence."

Like abolition lecturers, women's rights speakers often faced hecklers and hostile crowds. Sometime men interrupted with boos, hisses, or laughter. They threw rotten eggs and even books at the speaker. Many people still disapproved of women speaking before mixed audiences. Others rejected the radical idea of women being equal to men.

AIN'T I A WOMAN?

Another speaker on the lecture circuit was Sojourner Truth. Born around 1797, she grew up as a slave in New York's Hudson River Valley. At the time she was called Isabella. She was freed from slavery by the New York Emancipation Act of 1827. In 1843, she became a Protestant preacher. And she took a new name: Sojourner Truth.

Truth traveled and lectured throughout the eastern United States. She shared her experiences as a slave. And she called for the abolishment of slavery. She also spoke in favor of equal rights for women.

In May 1851 Sojourner Truth appeared at the Ohio Woman's Rights Convention in Akron. There, she delivered a powerful speech. It was later published under the name, "Ain't I a

Sojourner Truth (1797?–1883) became famous for denouncing slavery and for encouraging male legislators to give women the right to vote.

FAST FACT

Sojourner Truth could not read or write. She dictated her life story to Olive Gilbert. The resulting book, *The Narrative of Sojourner Truth*, was published in 1850.

Woman?" Truth pointed out that as a slave she had worked as hard as a man. "I have plowed and reaped and husked and chopped and mowed. Can any man do more than that?" she asked. She insisted that she did the same work as men. So she should receive the same rights as men.

PETITION CAMPAIGNS

One way women worked for equal rights was through petition campaigns. They were usually timed to coincide with revisions of state constitutions. Petitions were scheduled for delivery to state legislators in time to influence debates.

Suffrage petitions sometimes simply called for the removal of the word "male" from a constitution's statement on suffrage. Other petitions called for rewriting laws. They were more complicated. A major goal in every state was to change laws that took away married women's rights.

Abolition women were familiar with petitioning. But equal rights and suffrage for women were not popular issues. Most people refused to sign or even open their doors to suffrage workers.

PUBLICATIONS AND NEWSPAPERS

Some newspapers were friendly to the cause. They included Garrison's *Liberator*, the *Frederick Douglass Paper*, and the *New York Tribune*. These papers published the minutes of women conventions. They also printed letters and essays by activists.

(Right) Paulina Wright Davis (1813–1876) was editor of *The Una* from 1853 to 1855. A well-known speaker and abolitionist, she organized the 1850 National Women's Rights Convention in Worcester, Massachusetts, and delivered the keynote address.

Two women's newspapers gave the movement publicity. One publication was *The Lily*, published in Seneca Falls. Amelia Jenks Bloomer served as its editor. *The Lily* was founded in 1849 as a temperance paper. But it soon covered women's issues as well.

The first newspaper founded specifically to promote woman's rights was *The Una*. Editor Paulina Wright Davis launched the paper in February 1853. It was based in Providence, Rhode Island. The masthead proclaimed *The Una's* purpose: "A Paper Devoted to the Elevation of Woman."

Contributors to *The Lily* included Elizabeth Cady Stanton and Martha Wright. Stanton also wrote for *The Una*. Common topics included the female intellect, moral education, employment, and married women's property rights.

Female journalist Amelia Jenks Bloomer is best known for promoting the pantaloons and short skirt outfit that became known as the Bloomer (pictured). It was a much more comfortable outfit than the traditional full-length skirt and laced corsets worn by 19th-century women.

A VALUABLE PARTNERSHIP

Susan B. Anthony

In 1851 Susan B. Anthony traveled to Seneca Falls. The antislavery and temperance activist planned to attend some lectures. While in the town, Anthony was introduced to Elizabeth Cady Stanton. The two women soon developed a close friendship.

Stanton and Anthony began working together for various causes. One was the temperance movement. In 1852 the male-only temperance society would not allow Anthony to speak at a meeting. In frustration she decided to found her own society. That year she and Stanton formed the Woman's New York State Temperance Society. They launched a petition campaign. It called for a state law to abolish the sale of alcohol. In January 1853 they submitted documents with 28,000 signatures.

The two women also campaigned to change property laws for married women. The New York law passed in 1848 had many holes. Stanton and Anthony called for a new law. This one would give married women the right to their own wages. It would give them guardianship of their children. It would guarantee many other legal rights.

To promote passage of the new law, Anthony traveled a wide lecture circuit. She arranged meetings. And she traveled throughout the state. She

FAST FACT

A good friend of Lucy Stone at Oberlin College was Antoinette Louisa Brown (1825–1921). She was one of the first ordained ministers in the nation. She also lectured in favor of women's suffrage. In January 1856, Brown married Lucy's brother-in-law Samuel Charles Blackwell.

HELPING SLAVES TO ESCAPE

In 1850 Congress passed the Fugitive Slave Act. It required people in Northern states to return escaped slaves. It also punished anyone who helped runaway slaves. The law angered abolitionists. Many became involved with the Underground Railroad. This secret network of people provided food and shelter to slaves traveling to freedom in Canada.

The free African Americans and white reformers who ran the Underground Railroad used railroad terms. Fugitives were referred to as "passengers." They were provided with food and shelter at "stations." And a "conductor" led them from one station to the next.

An estimated 50,000 to 100,000 black slaves made their way to freedom through the Underground Railroad. One of the conductors, Harriet Tubman, was

Harriet Tubman

herself an escaped slave. During the 1850s she helped about 300 slaves to freedom. She also lectured at antislavery conventions and on women's rights.

put up posters and gave lectures. Stanton did not join her. Family demands kept her from giving many speeches. But she wrote speeches that Anthony delivered. It took many years. But in 1860 the New York State legislature finally passed the new law.

Throughout the 1850s, Stanton had many family obligations. By May 1853, she had five children. By 1859, she had seven. It was hard to find the time to write. To give Stanton the chance to work, Anthony would help with the children. The writing itself was often a team effort. Stanton crafted the articles or lectures, and Anthony critiqued them. "In writing we did better work together than either could alone," Elizabeth would later say.

NATIONAL CONVENTIONS

The women's rights movement did not have nationally elected officers. A central committee put together national conventions. Among the members were Antoinette Brown Blackwell, William H. Channing, Paulina Wright Davis, Abby K. Foster, Elizabeth Cady Stanton, Lucretia Mott, and Lucy Stone.

The first two national conventions, held in 1850 and 1851, took place in Worcester. During the next several years, the location varied. The 1852 convention was held in Syracuse, New York. Susan B. Anthony would later say that Lucy Stone's speech in Syracuse converted her to work for women's rights. The fourth convention was held in Cleveland, Ohio. The fifth meeting took place in Philadelphia. The sixth convention, held in 1855, was in Cincinnati, Ohio.

New York City was the site for the next four National Women's Rights Conventions. They were held in 1856, 1858, 1859, and 1860. The May 1860 event was the first national convention that Elizabeth Cady Stanton attended. Family duties had kept her away from the previous national meetings. She was now ready to do more for the movement. But the country's attention would soon be directed elsewhere.

6

CIVIL WAR

Disagreements over slavery had plagued the United States for decades. Finally, it tore the nation apart. By February 1861, seven Southern states had seceded from the United States. They formed a new nation. It was called the Confederate States of America. A month later Abraham Lincoln became the U.S. president.

On the morning of April 12, 1861, Confederate forces attacked the Union stronghold of Fort Sumter. War between the North and the South had begun. Soon after, four more Southern states joined the Confederacy.

Each side assumed it would claim a quick victory. But the Civil War would stretch for four years of bloody combat. More than 600,000 Americans would lose their lives.

SUPPORTING THE WAR

While their men were at war, women took care of the day-to-day operation of plantations, farms, and businesses. In both the North and the South they formed volunteer aid societies. These groups raised funds for soldiers' food, clothing, and medical supplies. The societies also organized women to sew, knit, and roll bandages.

Southern women suffered great hardships during the war. Most battles took place within the Confederate states. Women who lived near battlefields saw violent fighting. After conflicts, they tended to the dead and dying. Some watched as Union troops looted and destroyed their homes. As the war dragged on, life became even harder in the South. Roads and railroads were blocked, so people struggled with shortages of food and other necessities.

Life also changed in the North. But for many women, the change meant greater independence. During the war Northern women took some of the jobs previously held by men. Some women had clerical jobs with government agencies. Others worked as seamstresses in garment factories. These factories churned out uniforms, tents, and other military supplies.

NURSING

In both the North and the South, thousands of women became nurses. Before the war, nursing was a man's job. But medical care was desperately needed. Many women volunteered to help. At first, the Union turned to Dorothea Dix to organize nursing volunteers. She was named the superintendent of women nurses. During the war, Clara Barton earned a reputation for organizing nursing care on the battlefields.

In New York, health reformer and physician Elizabeth Blackwell helped create and train a nursing corps of women volunteers. It was called the Woman's Central Association for Relief. Blackwell's program was replaced in time by the U.S. Sanitary Commission. The Washington, D.C.–based agency coordinated the volunteer efforts of women working to support the war.

FAST FACT

In both the North and the South, women quickly committed to the war effort. Within two weeks of the attack on Fort Sumter, there were an estimated 20,000 local aid societies.

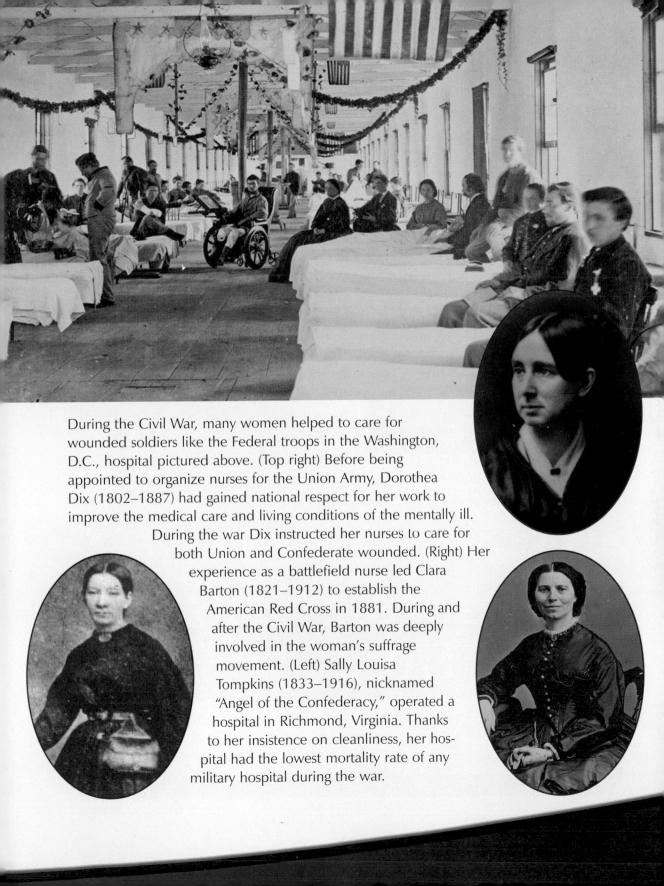

During the Civil War, many women helped to care for wounded soldiers like the Federal troops in the Washington, D.C., hospital pictured above. (Top right) Before being appointed to organize nurses for the Union Army, Dorothea Dix (1802–1887) had gained national respect for her work to improve the medical care and living conditions of the mentally ill. During the war Dix instructed her nurses to care for both Union and Confederate wounded. (Right) Her experience as a battlefield nurse led Clara Barton (1821–1912) to establish the American Red Cross in 1881. During and after the Civil War, Barton was deeply involved in the woman's suffrage movement. (Left) Sally Louisa Tompkins (1833–1916), nicknamed "Angel of the Confederacy," operated a hospital in Richmond, Virginia. Thanks to her insistence on cleanliness, her hospital had the lowest mortality rate of any military hospital during the war.

During the Civil War, Dr. Mary Edward Walker (1832–1919) worked as a battlefield surgeon for the Union Army. For her service she received the Medal of Honor—the only woman ever to earn the U.S. military's highest award for bravery. After the war, Walker wrote and lectured about women's rights and health care.

There were several thousand local branches of the U.S. Sanitary Commission. Some women ran fundraisers for their local organization. The money was used to purchase military supplies. Other women collected blankets and other supplies for soldiers. Still others served as army nurses. They were assigned to field hospitals by the Commission. The experiences gained in nursing led many women to establish careers in medicine.

LECTURING

The 11th National Women's Rights Convention had been scheduled for the spring of 1861. Susan B. Anthony urged her fellow reformers to hold the

FAST FACT

In 1849 Elizabeth Blackwell (1821–1910) became one of the first female doctors in the United States. In 1857 she founded the New York Infirmary for Women and Children.

In 1864, Anna Elizabeth Dickinson (1842–1932) became the first woman to speak before the U.S. Congress. Her speech received a standing ovation. During the 1860s and 1870s, Dickinson spoke often about slavery (and later, about the rights of newly freed African Americans), as well as on women's suffrage, issues related to Reconstruction, and temperance.

meeting. But she could not convince them. For four years, no national women's rights meetings were held. And no petition campaigns went forward.

Women's rights activists continued to lecture during the war. But they spoke as abolitionists. There was a new face on the antislavery lecture circuit. Anna Dickinson was just 19 years old when she first captured the attention of audiences. The abolitionist lecturer also found success talking politics. She was so effective that Republican groups hired her. In 1863 she gave speeches for Republican election campaigns in New Hampshire, Connecticut, and Pennsylvania. Dickinson even delivered a speech before the U.S. House of Representatives.

Dickinson would later lecture on suffrage for women. But in the early 1860s her emphasis was abolition and politics. Such subjects had been previously been considered unsuitable for a woman.

WOMAN'S NATIONAL LOYAL LEAGUE

On January 1, 1863, Abraham Lincoln signed the Emancipation Proclamation. It proclaimed freedom for blacks living in the Confederate states. Elizabeth Cady Stanton and Susan B. Anthony were disturbed that the Emancipation Proclamation did not do more. It did not end slavery in the border states that were still part of the Union.

In April 1863 Stanton and Anthony founded a new group called the Woman's National Loyal League. Elizabeth described the WNLL as "the first and only organization of women for the declared purpose of influencing politics." Among the group's officers and members were Stanton, Anthony, Lucy Stone, and Angelina Grimké Weld.

The following month the first WNLL meeting was held in New York City. At the meeting, Anthony presented a resolution on women's rights. It read, "There never can be a true peace in this Republic until the civil and political rights of all citizens of African descent and all women are practically established." But the delegates would not approve it. Leaders of the women's rights movement had agreed to stop activities until the war's end.

SUSAN B. ANTHONY (1820–1906)

Susan Brownell Anthony was born in Adams, Massachusetts, on February 15, 1820. Raised in the Quaker faith, she grew up believing men and women were equals. In 1837 the Anthony family moved to Rochester, New York. There, they were active in the antislavery movement.

Susan attended a Quaker seminary in Philadelphia. Afterward, she worked as a schoolteacher. During that time she campaigned at teachers' conventions for better pay for female teachers.

In 1849 Anthony retired from teaching. She became a lecturer for the temperance movement. In 1852 she and Elizabeth Cady Stanton founded the Woman's New York State Temperance Society.

Anthony campaigned for many other issues. She lobbied to change New York State laws to give married women more legal rights. And she gave lectures on abolition. The American Anti-Slavery Society hired her as an agent in 1856.

But Susan B. Anthony is best known for her efforts to win women the right to vote. In a partnership with Elizabeth Cady Stanton, she worked for more than 50 years for women's suffrage. Anthony died in 1906. It would be 14 years before the 19th Amendment was passed and ratified. It grants women the right to vote. It is also known as the Susan B. Anthony amendment.

A resolution that was approved involved petitioning. The women called on Congress to pass a Constitutional amendment abolishing slavery. They planned to gather a million signatures to support that demand.

THE SACRED RIGHT TO PETITION

As WNLL secretary, Anthony organized the petition drive. In December 1863 she noted that petitioning was women's only means for political power. They could not vote. They could not serve in the military. "Women can neither take the ballot nor the bullet to settle this question [of slavery]," Anthony said. "Therefore to us, the right to petition is the one sacred right which we ought not to neglect."

In 1864 petitions bearing 400,000 signatures were presented to Congress. The following January Congress passed the Thirteenth Amendment to the Constitution. It abolished slavery. In December 1865, the amendment was ratified and became federal law.

UNIVERSAL SUFFRAGE

On April 9, 1865, the Civil War ended. On that date General Robert E. Lee surrendered to Ulysses S. Grant at Appomattox, Virginia. Just five days later President Lincoln was assassinated. A shocked nation looked to a new president, Andrew Johnson.

During the war, women had stopped working to obtain the vote. Now that the war was over, Elizabeth Cady Stanton spoke up. In a July 1865 newspaper article, she appealed for women's suffrage. "No country ever has had or ever will have peace until every citizen has a voice in the government," she wrote. "Now let us try universal suffrage." Universal suffrage referred to the right to vote for all men and women, black and white. In the fall of 1865 Susan B. Anthony and Lucy Stone began to organize a petition drive.

But abolition groups were focused on obtaining voting rights for freed black men. Abolitionists Wendell Phillips and Charles Sumner asked that the woman suffrage question be put aside. They believed that achieving suffrage for black men was more important.

CITIZENSHIP AND VOTING RIGHTS

In late 1865 two amendments to the U.S. Constitution were proposed. The Fourteenth Amendment was to protect the right of citizenship of freed blacks. Its first paragraph notes, "all persons born or naturalized in the United States . . . are citizens." It goes on to specify the word "male" in describing who can vote. The Fifteenth Amendment stated that the right to vote could not be denied "on account of race, color, or previous condition of servitude." It did not refer to gender.

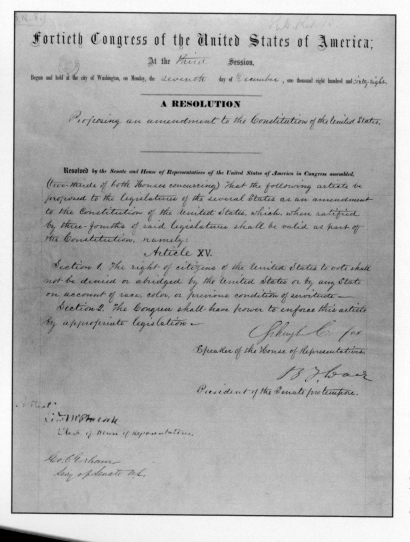

The Fifteenth Amendment to the U.S. Constitution, passed by Congress on February 26, 1869, and ratified on February 3, 1870, granted African-American men the right to vote. Female abolitionists had played a major role in the amendment's passage. However, an amendment to the Constitution that would guarantee women the right to vote would not come for another 50 years.

FAST FACT

Only one woman who signed the 1848 Declaration of Sentiments, Charlotte Woodward, would be alive in 1920, when women finally won the right to vote.

Women wanted universal suffrage. They worked to have the amendments changed to give women and blacks the vote at the same time. Activists gathered signatures on "A Petition for Universal Suffrage." And Congressman Thaddeus Stevens submitted the petition. But no amendments that provided universal suffrage were passed.

TAKING STOCK

Women had not won the right to vote by the mid-1860s. But their reform efforts had improved their lives and those of their sisters. Girls had more opportunities for a better education. In some states, married woman were guaranteed legal rights to property. And in a few places, widowed women had the right to vote—at least in school board elections.

But women still had a long way to go. More than 50 years would pass before they could legally cast a ballot in a national election. There would be lengthy delays and divisions. But the way forward was clear. Women were citizens of the United States. And they were entitled to the right to vote.

CHAPTER NOTES

p. 9:   "We abolition women are . . ." Angelina Grimké, quoted in Catherine H. Birney, *The Grimké Sisters, Sarah and Angelina Grimké* (Cirencester, England: Echo Library, 2005), 118.

p. 10:   "In marriage husband and . . ." William Blackstone, quoted in Roy Porter, *English Society in the Eighteenth Century* (New York, Penguin, 1990), 24.

p. 11:   "Who can look without disgust . . ." Catharine Beecher, quoted in Gail Collins, *American Women: 400 Years of Dolls, Drudges, Helpmates, and Heroines* (New York: William Morrow, 2003), 99.

p. 11:   "I stand before you . . ." Angelina Grimké, quoted in Gerda Lerner, *The Grimké Sisters from South Carolina: Pioneers for Woman's Rights* (New York, Oxford University Press, 1998), 8.

p. 12:   "American women have to do . . ." Angelina Grimké, quoted in Lerner, *The Grimké Sisters from South Carolina*, 8.

p. 21:   "grew up so thoroughly imbued . . ." Lucretia Mott, quoted in Sally G. McMillen, *Seneca Falls and the Origins of the Women's Rights Movement* (New York: Oxford University Press, 2008), 35.

p. 23:   "There would be but . . ." Congressman Walker, quoted in Lerner, *The Grimké Sisters from South Carolina*, 205.

p. 27:   "The appropriate duties . . . her character becomes unnatural." Pastoral Letter of the General Association of the Congregational Churches of Massachusetts, quoted in Larry Ceplair, *The Public Years of Sarah and Angelina Grimké* (New York: Columbia University Press, 1989), 211.

p. 28:   "I ask no favors . . ." Sarah Grimké, *Letters on the Equality of the Sexes*, quoted in Elizabeth Frost-Knappman and Kathryn Cullen-Dupont, *Women's Suffrage in America* (New York: Facts on File, 2005), 35.

p. 28:   "What then can woman . . ." Angelina Grimké, quoted in Lerner, *The Grimké Sisters from South Carolina*, 152.

p. 28:   "The investigation of the rights . . ." Angelina Grimké, *Letters to Catherine E. Beecher in Reply to an Essay on Slavery and Abolitionism Addressed to A. E. Grimké*, Boston: Isaac Knap, 1838, 114.

p. 31:   "would lower the dignity . . ." Lucretia Mott, quoted in Frost-Knappman and Cullen-Dupont, *Women's Suffrage in America*, 58.

p. 31:   "As Mrs. Mott and I . . ." Stanton, quoted in Collins, *American Women*, 113.

p. 33: "A Convention to discuss . . ." Elizabeth Cady Stanton, Susan B. Anthony, and Matilda Joslyn Gage, eds., *History of Woman Suffrage*, Vol. 1, 1848–1861 (Rochester, N.Y.: Charles Mann, 1889), 67.

p. 34: "We hold these truths . . . Stanton, Anthony, Gage, *History of Woman Suffrage*, Vol. 1, 70.

p. 36: "Resolved, that it is . . ." Stanton, Anthony, Gage, *History of Woman Suffrage*, Vol. 1, 72.

p. 36: "But I persisted, for . . ." Elizabeth Cady Stanton, quoted in Theodore Stanton and Harriot Stanton Blatch, eds. *Elizabeth Cady Stanton: As Revealed in Her Letters, Diaries and Reminiscences*, Vol. 1 (New York: Harper and Brothers, 1922), 146.

p. 38: "degraded into a mere dependent," Lucretia Mott, quoted in McMillen, *Seneca Falls and the Origins*, 100.

p. 39: "employ agents, circulate tracts . . ." Stanton, Anthony, Gage, *History of Woman Suffrage*, Vol. 1, 71.

p. 40: "I was a woman . . ." Lucy Stone, quoted in Carol Lasser and Marlene Deahl Merrill, eds. *Friends and Sisters: Letters Between Lucy Stone and Antoinette Brown Blackwell, 1846–93* (Urbana: University of Illinois, 1987), 12.

p. 41: "Wherever she goes . . ." Lucy Stone, quoted in Andrea Moore Kerr, *Lucy Stone: Speaking Out for Equality* (Piscataway, N.J.: Rutgers University Press, 1992), 50.

p. 42: "I have plowed . . ." Sojourner Truth, quoted in Carleton Mabee and Susan Mabee Newhouse, *Sojourner Truth: Slave, Prophet, Legend* (New York: New York University Press, 1995), 81.

p. 43: "A Paper Devoted . . ." McMillen, *Seneca Falls and the Origins*, 134.

p. 46: "In writing we did . . ." Elizabeth Cady Stanton, quoted in McMillen, *Seneca Falls and the Origins*, 109.

p. 52: "the first and only . . ." Elizabeth Cady Stanton, quoted in McMillen, *Seneca Falls and the Origins*, 155.

p. 52: "There never can be . . ." Susan B. Anthony, quoted in Mari Jo Buhle and Paul Buhle, eds. *The Concise History of Woman Suffrage* (Champaign: University of Illinois Press, 2005), 199.

p. 53: "Women can neither take . . ." Susan B. Anthony, quoted in Wendy Hamand Venet, *Neither Ballots nor Bullets: Women Abolitionists and the Civil War* (Charlottesville: University of Virginia Press, 1991), 94.

p. 53: "No country ever has . . ." Elizabeth Cady Stanton, quoted in McMillen, *Seneca Falls and the Origins*, 160.

CHRONOLOGY

1821: Emma Hart Willard founds the Troy Female Seminary in New York.

1833: Lucretia Mott founds the Philadelphia Female Anti-Slavery Society; Oberlin College is founded.

1836: Angelina Grimké and her sister Sarah Grimké begin speaking publicly against slavery.

1837: The first National Female Anti-Slavery Society Convention is held in New York City; Mary Lyon founds Mount Holyoke College in Massachusetts; Oberlin College begins admitting women.

1839: The American Anti-Slavery Society votes to allow women as full members in the organization.

1840: Lucretia Mott, Elizabeth Cady Stanton, and other women are not allowed to participate in the World Anti-Slavery Convention held in London.

1848: On July 19, the first women's rights convention is held in Seneca Falls, New York.

1850: Lucretia Mott publishes *Discourse on Woman*; the first national convention on women's rights is held in Worcester, Massachusetts.

1851: Sojourner Truth gives a powerful speech entitled "Ain't I a Woman?"

1852: Stanton, Anthony, and others found the Women's New York State Temperance Society.

1861: Civil War begins; activities of the suffrage movement stop as women support the war effort.

1863: President Lincoln signs the Emancipation Proclamation; Stanton, Anthony, and others found the first national women's organization, the Woman's National Loyal League.

1865: Civil War ends; in December, the Thirteenth Amendment, which abolishes slavery, is ratified.

GLOSSARY

abolitionist—a member of the movement to abolish, or put an end to, slavery.

advocate—to speak in support of.

amendment—a legal change to the U.S. Constitution.

discourse—a formal discussion of a topic in a speech.

emancipate—to set free.

guardianship—the legal responsibility and authority to care for someone.

lobby—to try to influence politicians or public officials about a particular issue.

radical—extreme.

reform—to bring about beneficial change in an institution in order to improve it; to abolish injustice.

resolution—a formal expression of intentions, as determined by a vote at a political meeting.

secede—to break away from.

temperance—the practice of refraining from drinking alcohol.

tract—a pamphlet or booklet published on political or religious issues.

FURTHER READING

FOR YOUNGER READERS

Burgan, Michael. *Elizabeth Cady Stanton: Social Reformer*. Mankato, Minn.: Compass Point Books, 2006.

Colman, Penny. *Elizabeth Cady Stanton and Susan B. Anthony: A Friendship That Changed the World*. New York: Henry Holt, 2011.

Crewe, Sabrina, and Dale Anderson. *The Seneca Falls Women's Rights Convention*. Milwaukee: Gareth Stevens, 2005.

Hopkinson, Deborah. *Susan B. Anthony: Fighter for Women's Rights*. New York: Aladdin, 2005.

Marsico, Katie. *Lucretia Mott*. Minneapolis, Minn.: Abdo Publishing, 2008.

McNeese, Tim. *The Abolitionist Movement: Ending Slavery*. New York: Chelsea House, 2007.

FOR OLDER READERS

Lerner, Gerda. *The Grimké Sisters from South Carolina: Pioneers for Women's Rights and Abolition*. Chapel Hill: University of North Carolina Press, 2009.

McMillen, Sally G. *Seneca Falls and the Origins of the Women's Rights Movement*. New York: Oxford University Press, 2008.

INTERNET RESOURCES

http://ecssba.rutgers.edu/

The Elizabeth Cody Stanton & Susan B. Anthony Papers Project provides links to the writings of both Stanton and Anthony.

http://greatwomen.org/

The website for the National Women's Hall of Fame, located in Seneca Falls, New York, features biographies of American women who have made major contributions in U.S. history.

www.nps.gov/wori

This National Park Service website for the Women's Rights National Historical Park provides background information on the first women's rights convention in Seneca Falls, New York.

www.nwhm.org/online-exhibits/rightsforwomen/index.html

The National Women's History Museum features an exhibit on the women's suffrage movement. It includes links to information on the abolition movement and the Seneca Falls Convention.

www.pbs.org/stantonanthony/

The PBS-sponsored website for the film *Not for Ourselves Alone: The Story of Elizabeth Cady Stanton and Susan B. Anthony* provides biographical information on the two women. And it features historical documents about and essays on the women's movement.

INDEX

Numbers in **bold italics** refer to captions.

CONTRIBUTORS

LeeAnne Gelletly is the author of several books for young adults, including biographies of Harriet Beecher Stowe, Mae Jemison, Roald Dahl, Ida Tarbell, and John Marshall.

Senior Consulting Editor **A. Page Harrington** is executive director of the Sewall-Belmont House and Museum, on Capitol Hill in Washington, D.C. The Sewall-Belmont House celebrates women's progress toward equality—and explores the evolving role of women and their contributions to society—through educational programs, tours, exhibits, research and publications.

The historic National Woman's Party (NWP), a leader in the campaign for equal rights and women's suffrage, owns, maintains, and interprets the Sewall-Belmont House and Museum. One of the premier women's history sites in the country, this National Historic Landmark houses an extensive collection of suffrage banners, archives, and artifacts documenting the continuing effort by women and men of all races, religions, and backgrounds to win voting rights and equality for women under the law.

The Sewall-Belmont House and Museum and the National Woman's Party are committed to preserving the legacy of Alice Paul, founder of the NWP and author of the Equal Rights Amendment, and telling the untold stories for the benefit of scholars, current and future generations of Americans, and all the world's citizens.